WINDMILLS

WINDMILLS

SALLY TAYLOR

TODTRI

PICTURE CREDITS

Mary Evans Picture Library
7, 9, 10, 11, 15, 16, 22, 23, 40, 42,
51 (top & bottom), 61

Images Colour Library
28/29 (ICL), 34 & 35 (David Barnes), 54/55
(Gavin Hellier)

Ronald Pearsall
26, 50 (right)

Picture Perfect (New York)
6, 8, 12/13, 17, 18/19. 20, 31, 36/37, 52, 60, 64,
69, 70/71, 76/77

Sally Taylor
14, 24, 25, 27, 30, 32, 35, 41, 43, 44, 45, 46/47,
48, 49, 50 (left), 53, 56, 57, 58, 62, 63, 65, 66,
67, 68, 74, 75

This book was designed and produced by
TODTRI Book Publishers
P.O. Box 572, New York, NY 10116-0572
Fax: (212) 695-6984
e-mail: todtri@mindspring.com

Printed and bound in Singapore

ISBN 1-57717-158-6

Visit us on the web!
www.todtri.com

Author: Sally Taylor

Publisher: Robert M. Tod
Editor: Nicolas Wright
Art Directorr: Ron Pickless
Typesetting & DTP: Blanc Verso UK

CONTENTS

INTRODUCTION

"I can think of few merrier spectacles than that of many windmills bickering together in a fresh breeze in a wooded country, their halting alacrity of movement, their pleasant business making bread all day long with uncouth gesticulations, their air gigantically human as of a creature half alive."

So wrote Robert Louis Stevenson in the second half of the nineteenth century, when in some places traditional windmills had already begun their decline. For close on 700 years, they had been a focal point of the landscape; whether they stood high on a hill or towered above nearby buildings so as to catch the wind, windmills have always somehow both dominated and harmonised with the surrounding scene.

Their importance and the respect paid them through the ages doubtless had something to do with the fact they were producing the most staple of foods. So long as the sails of the windmill were turning, flour was being milled and bread could be baked. They were the embodied response to '*Give us this day our daily bread*'.

That they were both revered and a symbol of comfort and familiarity is apparent in the frequency with which they occur in paintings through their history. A depiction of the discovery of the infant Moses has a windmill in it, although such a scene was long before their time; famous artists – Gainsborough, Rembrandt, Breughel the elder, John Constable and William Turner – all recognised the appeal of the windmill and often included them in their pictures.

The 'human air' that Stevenson alludes to led people to ascribe a living soul or spirit to windmills. Anyone who demolished a windmill, it was thought, would encounter bad luck. Like those other great wind-powered structures, sailing ships, a windmill is nearly always female – a notable exception being one on the Sussex Downs in England which is called Jack. It stands in close proximity to another earlier mill, named Jill – perhaps it was considered at the time that two females could not work together so closely in harmony!

In Holland, particularly, where windmills had such significance, they were given names – The Cat, Lion, Stalk, Seagull, Cornflower, Prince's Garden. The proud miller would have plaques, known as beards, carved in wood which were nailed to the bottom of the cap beneath the sails; often these were copied into the coats of arms of knighted families. In the UK, they more frequently took the name of the miller, leading to inevitable confusion when a new one took over. Often they were known prosaically as black mill or white mill according to the colour they were painted.

The windmill as 'human' was taken to its extreme by Cervantes romantic hero,

Don Quixote. Coming across a collection of windmills on the Spanish plains, he declared they were 'giants, two leagues in length or more' and charged towards them at full gallop with his lance; this caught in a sail and lifted Quixote and his horse clean off the ground. *'To tilt at windmills'* has thus come to mean silly behaviour, likely to end in ridicule.

Left: Like many creative artists, Robert Louis Stevenson, the nineteenth-century author and great traveller , found the sight of windmills in the English landscape profoundly nostalgic and moving.

Previous pages left: A windmill in the Canary Island of Lanzarote. Catching the strong winds from the Atlantic, windmills worked efficiently and long played an important part of daily life in on these Spanish islands.

Previous pages right: An illustration by French artist Gustave Dore of Don Quixote who gave us the phrase 'tilting at windmills'. It came from the story of how he spurred on his horse to charge at windmills espied across the Spanish plains, believing them to be 'giants, two leagues in length or more'.

In the words at the top of the page taken from 'The Foreigner at Home', Stevenson describes how his traveller sees at 'the end of airy vistas the revolution of the windmill sails'. and adds, "he may go where he pleases in the future, he may see Alps, and pyramids, and lions, but it will be hard to beat the pleasure of that moment".

In this book we pay tribute to 'that moment' – to the windmills of the past that were so important to our ancestors. Let's hope the few that are left, dotted here and there in our countrysides, will continue to grace landscapes for years to come.

WINDMILL SAYINGS AND SUPERSTITIONS

The importance, yet familiarity, of windmills in bygone days is apparent from the number of sayings related to them that we include in our everyday conversation today.

TO HAVE WINDMILLS IN YOUR HEAD

This means to have a head full of fancies. It follows Don Quixote's actions in the episode mentioned in the introduction. His companion, Sancho Panchez, says, "Did I not tell your worship they were windmills? And who could have thought otherwise, except such as had windmills

in their head?" Centuries later, the film *Thomas Crown Affair* featured a title song following this theme – *The Windmills of your Mind*, which became a classic.

GRIST TO THE MILL

Grist was the corn that came into the mill to be ground. The phrase therefore originally meant work undertaken for profit; nowadays it is often used simply to mean work that needs to be done.

Above: A portrait of the eighteenth-century artist John Constable, possibly England's finest landscape painter.
Many of his paintings depicted windmills.

Opposite: A charming lithograph of an early nineteenth-century windmill, by an unknown artist.

RUN OF THE MILL

This probably comes from the textile mills in the first instance and means anything that is ordinary and routine. Such, however, is the work of all mills – a run referred to the period when a mill was working.

TO GO THROUGH THE MILL

To endure some particularly hard or arduous experience. Anything that went through the mill – corn, wood, groundnuts – had its character fundamentally changed.

A MILLSTONE AROUND ONE'S NECK

The reference to this – meaning anything or anyone that acts as a debilitating encumbrance – actually predates windmills, coming as it does from the Bible.

'Whoso shall offend one of these little ones which believe in me, it were better for him that a millstone were hanged about his neck, and that he were drowned in the depth of the sea'.

Millstones carry their own superstitions. It is not unusual to see millstones in graveyards; if a miller was fataly injured, the millstones were considered unlucky and would never be used again.

Left: A blazing sun gives a glorious backcloth to these Dutch windmills disapearing into the distance at the end of a long summers' day.

CHAPTER ONE

WINDMILL BEGINNINGS

The exact date when man thought of harnessing wind power to grind the corn for his daily bread – and so built the first windmill – is lost in the mists of antiquity. Clearly he had already recognised the power that abounded in the air, for he had long since built sailing ships to catch the wind that blew across rivers and oceans. Equally, we know he had devised and constructed watermills to turn heavy millstones for milling flour some time before windmills came into being.

One of the earliest authenticated record comes from two tenth century Arab writers, Al-Mas'udi and Al-Istahri, who wrote of windmills in Seistan, a dry land way above sea level on the borders of Iran – Persia as it was then – and Afghanistan. These mills, it seems, were used not for grinding flour, but for collecting water; the writings telling us that, "There the wind drives mills and raises water from the streams whereby gardens are irrigated".

There are sources that suggest an even earlier presence of windmills, one being the Hindu classic that dates from around the third century BC. It makes reference to water being raised 'by contrivances worked by wind-power'. An 1841 publication entitled *Millions of Facts*, claims that windmills

Above: Different types
of windmills apparent-
ly work in close
proximity in the rural
countryside of this
picture.

Previous pages left: A
convict built windmill,
now known simply as
the Old Windmill,
stands high on a hill in
Brisbane, Australia.

Previous pages right:
Some of the earliest
windmills in Europe
were built in France.
This one dates from
the mid-eighteenth
century

Opposite: An elegant
example of a Greek
windmill.

were first invented by Hero of Alexandria – the Greek scientist and mathematician who lived about the time of Christ. Another source cites a reference to a slave who told a seventh-century Caliph that he could construct a mill that would be turned by the wind. Two centuries later, an engineer in Baghdad referred to a fountain being worked by a wheel, 'like those which people are accustomed to install in *windmills*', thus apparently giving confirmation of their existence. Ninth-century Arabic writings also refer to a Persian millwright of the seventh century who worked a wind-driven grain mill.

If the exact date of their beginnings cannot be accurately pinpointed, it does, however, seem certain that in the earliest windmills the sails were set in a horizontal, rather than a vertical plane. They were attached onto a vertical shaft which ran straight up from the top – or *runner* – millstone and they were housed in a walled building with opposing gaps in the walls through which the wind was directed onto the driving side of the sails, causing them to turn. As millstones had so far been turned horizontally by human, animal or water force, this may perhaps have seemed the most logical setting of the sails when they were powered by the wind. On any one site in Seistan there would be numbers of such mills, sometimes as many as 75, the sails being con-

structed of reed mats or wickerwork.

It seems that this horizontal arrangement of the windmill extended mainly eastwards, apparently disseminated by the prisoners of Genghis Khan. The Chinese took the idea and built windmills for irrigation purposes, refining the construction by abandoning the outside walls and instead setting the sails at an angle to the vertical shaft so that they would catch the wind without the through draught from the openings in the walls.

Although the introduction of windmills into western and northern Europe is sometimes attributed to information brought back by Christians returning from the Crusades, the fact is that the appearance of the earliest known windmills in England and Europe differed radically from the horizontal mills. The first written record of a windmill in England dates to 1185 and refers to the renting of a mill in a Yorkshire village – let for an annual rent of 8 shillings. Before this time references to mills referred only to watermills or those driven by livestock – horses in particular.

Within the space of little more than 20 years, however, the windmill became a common sight around the countryside, although it was nearly a hundred years

Left: A group of Spanish windmills set alongside a rustic winding road.

before one appeared in an 'illuminated' manuscript – something that marked it as being generally familiar. The first such illustration was in the *English Windmill Psalter*, commonly dated at 1260. Purchased by William Morris at the end of the 19th century, this is now held in the Morgan Collection in the Pierpont Library in New York. Later, windmills are found carved around the exterior walls of churches and cloisters as well as into the arm ends of wooden pews, or decorating stained glass windows and memorial brasses. Miniature depictions of windmills appeared on the frontispiece illustration in fine English bibles and psalters.

Windmills seem to have spread quite rapidly through north and western Europe; there are certainly references to them in France in the twelfth century and they quickly spread to Germany and Switzerland. Interestingly, in the country most famed for windmills – Holland, known as the land of the windmills and whose national symbol is a windmill – the earliest record dates from the end of the thirteenth century. With few fast running streams or rivers crossing the countryside, it seems likely that Holland did not have the tradition of watermills that undoubtedly preceded windmills in many places.

It is a country that is perfectly suited to the windmill, however, being low-lying with a steady wind that blows steadfastly across the flat land. No wonder that that the art of building and working windmills was developed to its peak in Holland

It seems that it took a little longer for windmills to become established further south in Europe. The first windmills in Italy appeared at the end of the thirteenth/ early fourteenth century, but they did not become established in Spain and Portugal until some 100-200 years later. In Greece, they were first developed on the numerous islands where there was generally a lack of fast running water to power watermills but was, instead, a fairly reliable source of wind – frequent and generally steady. The appearance of the Greek island windmills, in particular, is markedly different from the windmills of northern Europe – they tend to be round, rather squat, circular buildings, usually whitewashed and generally with upwards of six triangular cloth sails spread on simple vanes.

The idea and construction of both watermills and traditional windmills travelled to the New World with the early settlers, amongst whom there were millers, just as there were all

Opposite: Windmills at La Mancha, Spain.

manner of skilled craftsmen. An early mill was built by the first colonial governor of Virginia, Sir George Yardley, who arrived there in 1610 after being shipwrecked off Bermuda. He was granted a 1000-acre plantation upon which he built a post mill.

By the mid-seventeenth century, windmills were operating in profusion in Massachusetts and New York, and, indeed, windmill sails formed part of the seal of New York. In 1680 there was a New York directive from the authorities to small craft that if the sails of the

prominent windmills had been taken in, no boat was to cross between New York and Brooklyn.

In their early days, mills in England were subject to *milling soke* rights – never the subject of an Act of Parliament as such, but part of the charter of each manor. Mills were generally owned by the lords of the manor, who leased them to the millers but retained an effective monopoly on their use. No mill could be built and set up in opposition to the manorial mill and all corn grown on the land belonging to the manor must be milled at the manorial mill, the miller taking payment – usually a proportion of the flour milled – for his services. If the lord of the manor wanted corn ground for his own use, this being done free, it would take precedent over everyone else's – even if the hoppers were already full of a tenant's grain.

In turn, the lord of the manor was supposed to provide and maintain sufficient mills to meet the demands of all his tenants. Should he demolish a mill or let one fall into such disrepair that it no longer worked, the *soke* was broken and the tenants could go elsewhere with their grain.

In the early days in the USA, such feudal practices had little place. Millers

Right: Windmills first appeared in America in the seventeenth century and were particularly prevalent along the eastern seaboard. This one dates from 1874.

Left: A detailed
etching by Dutch artist
Jan Van der Velde
shows a seventeenth-
century wip mill as
its most prominent
feature. Built as
pumping mills, wip
mills developed in
Holland and were also
known as hollow post
mills, as the drive
passed down through
the centre of the post to
gearing housed
beneath.

were favoured people with a standing in the community; food was an immediate and basic necessity of the early settlers and it was the miller alone who could easily produce the flour they needed for their daily bread if they were to be left free to cultivate the land. Not only were millers granted free land and guaranteed water rights, free labour was often provided to help build mills. Laws were passed to restrict the number of mills so that not too many would set up in opposition to one another and as mills were built, so communities would form around them.

In all places, doubtless because mills served such an important function and because almost everyone had to visit them regularly, they became very much the centres of communities, places where people would gather and meet, to exchange news and gossip. In some places they formed customs and traditions of their own; in many places they would be blessed by a priest at the beginning of each month or new season and millers would keep candles burning in nearby chapels and churches to ensure the patron saint would smile on them. When people bought their first grain of the year to be ground, they would often present the miller with an offering of food or wine. Thus the windmill was to become second only to the church as the focus of a community.

WINDMILL TYPES

T here are three types of traditional European windmill – namely the post mill, tower mill and smock mill in their basic form. The earliest of these was the post mill – the type of windmill that Sir George Yardley built on his Virginian plantation. Although its construction and workings are essentially simplistic, to label it simple is to do it an injustice – indeed in his book *Windmills and Watermills (1970)*, John Reynolds described as 'one of the most daring and ingenious works of the medieval carpenter'.

The post mill consisted of an upright rectan-

gular body, usually topped with a pointed roof, the entire structure of which pivoted on a single, massive, vertical post. This post, known simply as the *post*, was by far the largest timber in the post mill and extended about halfway up the body – or *buck* – of the mill, which was generally made of wood and was characteristically weatherboarded. The post was held in position by four sloping quarter bars, mortised into the post at their top end and held at their lower end on cross trees. The main post did not rest directly on the cross trees – instead it fitted into them and was thus held in position.

Initially this structure was buried in the ground to help keep it stable or left open to the elements. Finding that in either case, the wood would eventually rot, it was frequently lifted and supported on masonry piers. Later still these were all pro-

Above: Known as the 'Drug Mill of the Apothecaries' Company' this mill was a feature of the Lambeth skyline.

Previous pages left: The beautiful mellow brick tower mill at Billingford, Norfolk is understandably a well-known local landmark.

Previous pages right: Home to the oldest working post mill in England, Outwood in Surrey shows its heritage by depicting the mill on its village sign.

tected within roundhouse structures, many then being constructed beneath existing mills. Not only did they protect the timber from the worst of the weather, they also provided storage space for incoming grain and outgoing flour. They were built of wood, stone, bricks and clay and often had circular pitched roofs that might be boarded or, in some areas, thatched.

At the top of the post was the *crown tree*, another huge beam generally made of oak which rested across it. The *wind-shaft*, which supports the stocks on which the sails – or *sweeps* as they are known in some areas – were attached, initially passed horizontally into the top of the building. Before long, however, it was found to be more efficient if the wind-shaft was angled upwards slightly; the sails were then tilted clear of the body of the mill. On the opposite side to the sails was the door into the mill, often a stable door in post mills, possibly to let more light into the otherwise very gloomy building – the absence of glass, or its pro-

hibitive expense, in the early days meant there were only tiny openings for windows. The miller reached the door by climbing a ladder which was hinged at the top so that it could be lifted clear of the ground.

The reason for the huge central post extending up into the buck (and also why the ladder had to be lifted clear of the ground) can be found in the fact that a windmill's sails must face 'into the eye' of the prevailing wind if they were to catch it and thus turn. Because they were fixed

through into one side of the building in a post mill, it meant that the whole body of the mill had to be turned as the wind changed direction. To begin with, the miller would do this manually by pushing on the tailpole which was attached to the underneath of the buck, passing through the ladder and sloping down to the ground. Sometimes he might hitch his horse to the tailpole and lead it round the mill to turn the buck; in some mills the tailpole had a wheel at the end which ran in a grooved track round the mill, making

Dominating the hillocky common at Brill in the county of Buckinghamshire, England this post mill is the sole survivor of an original group of three. It dates from about 1680, was rebuilt 100 years later and has had various restorations during the twentieth century.

Left: Dutch windmills on the banks of the river.

this arduous job a little easier.

For a little over a hundred years in Europe the post mill was the only type of windmill. Then, perhaps because the effort required to turn the mill constricted its size and therefore how many sets of grinding stones it could house, at the beginning of the fourteenth century the tower mill appeared, the first one being built in France. As the name suggests these were essentially tall tower-like structures topped by a relatively small cap. The cap housed only the windshaft

and brake wheel and thus the sails and it was the only part of the structure that had to be turned into the wind.

The building itself, generally circular and tapering towards the top, was constructed of stone or brick and could be built much higher than a post mill, way above trees, for example, or other buildings, both of which, as time went on, would grow up around mills and impede the passage of the wind. The gearing and grinding machinery could be housed in the tower, which also had more room for

Above: One of Holland's most common, and yet picturesque, sights – a windmill by the side of a canal. Its function may have been to drain outlying land and maintain the water level in the canal.

Opposite: The handsome smock mill at Sarre, Kent is one of the few mills left in England that still operates commercially.

storage as well as space for more than one set of grinding stones. Where a post mill generally only had a couple of floors, a tower mill might have as many as four or five, sometimes more

The first tower mill appeared in England in the fifteenth century. It seems that the design led to the somewhat similar *smock mill*, which appeared here in the middle of the seventeenth century and quickly gained popularity. In this structure again, a comparatively small cap at the top of a fixed building housed the windshaft to which the sails were attached. The building itself, like the tower mill, was generally a much higher building than the post mill, and was most often octagonal in shape, although it could have six, ten or even twelve sides. It comprised a vertical timber frame that tapered towards the top and was clad with weatherboarding.

Smock mills were so called because they were said to look like a countryman – farmer or shepherd – in his traditional smock. Both tower and smock mills, incidentally, would always have two doors into the mill so that the miller, or anyone else who needed to, could get in and out of the mill whichever the sails were facing.

Caps were one of the distinguishing features of smock and tower mills and they varied in shape, generally according to areas. In the south east of England they were usually almost rectangular; in the midlands they were more frequently circular or ogee – that is formed by a concave curve tapering into a convex one which gives the cap a characteristic point. In the marshy country of south-east Anglia they often had the appearance of an upturned small rowing boat. Within different localities, many variations of each of these will be found.

The cap rested on the top of the mill in such a way that it could 'skid' easily around it, in either direction. Many were still turned by a tailpole or by pulling on a rope which ran over a wheel and down to the ground or a balcony, or *staging*, constructed a third or halfway way up some mills. In the middle of the eighteenth century, Englishman Edmund Lee made the whole process of turning the mill easier by the invention of the *fantail*. Known in some areas as a *fly tackle*, this comprised a wind-driven wheel of five to eight small vanes set either on the tailpole or the ladder of a post mill or on a cap in a tower or smock mill, always at right angles to the sails. As long as the sails

Opposite: The post mill at Outwood, Surrey is the oldest working post mill in England. It was built in 1665 and was restored to working order this century with the help of a grant from the Society for the Protection of Ancient Buildings who are constantly involved with windmill restoration and conservation.

Overleaf: Two of Holland's best known national symbols – a windmill and a field of tulips – make symbiotic partners.

were facing into the wind, the fantail kept still; if the wind moved round, it struck the vanes of the fantail, which would then revolve and cause the cap or the buck of the post mill to turn. Once again, the sails would be in the eye of the wind.

For some reason, this device subsequently widely used in England, never truly caught on throughout the Continent of Europe, particularly in Holland, where there were probably more windmills than anywhere. Here they continued to use the tailpole to turn the cap even on some of the huge mills.

The most common number of sails on a western or northern European windmill is four; those in Portugal Greece and Spain and their many islands often had a greater number, favouring 'jib' type sails like those of a sailing barge. Occasionally windmills were built with five or more sails, five apparently being very efficient in terms of working the mill. Such multi-sailed mills suffered less from the effects of one sail constantly being sheltered from the wind as it passed the building, but the disadvantage of an uneven number of sails was that if one broke, the mill would be unbalanced. If a sail broke or was damaged on a four, six or even eight-sailed

mill, its corresponding pair could be taken off and the mill could still function while repairs were undertaken. Eight sails were generally considered a maximum and were also quite rare – only about seven were known to have been built in the UK.

The design of sails has varied over

Above: Nutley mill, on the edge of Ashdown Forest – apparently the smallest post mill in England and also the only example of an open trestle mill in Sussex. At the time of this picture, she lacks one pair of sails.

Left: A peaceful and typically Dutch scene of windmills merging into the waterways and canal banks.

the centuries, many millers arriving at a new or adapted design as they worked. In the first instance, they generally comprised a simple wooden framework to which were attached a number of evenly spaced horizontal bars through which canvas was woven. The framework was flat but inclined at an angle to the direction of rotation.

Before long the sail frames were made more robust and had considerably more sail bars to support the canvas sails which overlaid them. Where the previous sails had been reefed to accommodate the strength of the wind by pulling them towards the middle like a curtain, now they had a greater number of adjustments. In a light wind, the full sail would be stretched over and attached to the frame. At least three other adjustments – *dagger* and *sword point* coming down to *first whip* or *reef* in a fierce wind – could be made. The frames were set onto the shaft with a slight twist, similar to the setting of blades on a propeller. Now known as common sails, the miller still had to adjust each sail individually and stop the mill working to make necessary adjustments if the strength of the wind altered.

In 1772 a Scotsman, Andrew Meikle,

invented the *spring sail*. Instead of canvas, each sail frame had a number of hinged shutters set into it, which opened and closed like those of a venetian blind. The shutters were controlled by a spring, the tension of which could be adjusted according to the power required. When the shutters were closed the sail offered a flat surface to the wind; as the wind pressure increased, so the shutters would hinge open to 'spill the wind'. Should the wind die down again, the tension on the spring once again pulled the shutters closed. The miller would still have to set the spring on each sail individually according to how he judged the strength of the wind.

Some 35 years later, Sir William Cubitt refined this invention producing the *patent sail*. Combining the shutters of the spring sail with a remote control chain mechanism, the sails could be adjusted simultaneously whilst still turning. Where before a miller would have to stop the mill to immobilise the sails before making individual adjustments, he could now make a simultaneous adjustment on all the sails as they were turning. Every such refinement made his task a little easier and the process of milling a little quicker.

Opposite: A classic Dutch windmill set against a foreground of reeds and graceful waterways.

CHAPTER THREE

WINDMILL WORKINGS

always produced their own 'labour-saving' devices whatever the walk of life. As a result there may have been slight variations from mill to mill. Basically, however windmills all worked in much the same way, the principle always being that the sails revolved in the wind and thereby turned the millstone or stones, so that grain may be ground into the flour.

The explanation given here of how a traditional grain mill works is extremely simplistic; to describe it in graphic engineering detail would take far too long. Some basic idea of how a windmill worked however adds greatly to an appreciation of these now rare and romantic buildings.

What the miller would hope for as he began work each day was a steady, constant wind, blowing about a force three or four. This achieves an entire revolution of the sails in approximately every four seconds, and from this he could probably produce about a ton of flour in some four to five hours.

The way a traditional grinding windmill works has always been comparatively simple, yet, like any simple invention, it is also ingenious. Obviously as decades wore on millers in different places added refinements to the workings of their mill, every generation having

When the mill is not working, the big, vertically positioned *brake wheel* inside the buck or cap, behind the sails, is stationary. To start the mill, the miller has to release the tension on this so that it can start turning. Either he or the fantail mechanism turns the sails into the eye of the wind and as the wind catches them, they will start to revolve.

The *windshaft*, to which the sails are attached, revolves with them. Presuming that the mill has patent sails the shutters on the sails will be closed as they start turning. When the sails have reached their maximum speed for milling, simple mechanisms come in to play, adjusting the shutters as the wind varies so as to keep the sails turning at that constant speed.

The teeth or cogs on the break wheel mesh into those on a smaller, horizontally placed wheel, known as the *wallower*. As it starts revolving, it turns the shaft at its centre that runs down through the mill to another horizontally placed wheel, bigger than the wallower, known as the *spur wheel*. In turn this meshes into one or more much small, horizontal wheels called *stone nuts*, the number varying according to how many pairs of stones the mill has and the miller wants to operate at any time. As they turn they

Above: An old windshaft lies on the ground. Constructed of wood or iron, the windshaft was the main axle running through the top of the mill to carry the sails and brake wheel.

Opposite: A whimsical French impression of a sixteenth-century windmill.

Previous pages left: An engraving by a French artist of a post mill.

Previous pages right: Prized now as decorative items, this millstone has been incorporated into a wall.

Above: The inside of
the cap at Sarre Mill.
The large vertical
wheel on the left is the
brake wheel; the hori-
zontal one on the right
is the wallower which
indirectly drives the
millstones.

rotate the spindle, on the end of which is the *runner* stone.

A post mill most often had only a ground and a first floor, storage being provided in the roundhouse below. A tower or smock mill would more fre-quently have three of four floors, so con-ditions are far less cramped. Grain would be hoisted up on a simple hoist, connected to the wallower, passing through trapdoors in the floors to the bin floor where it was tipped into storage bins. When milling started, grain would be poured into a hopper above the stones. It flowed down a chute from the bottom of the hopper to be directed onto the stones by a moving tray known as a *shoe*; simple mechanisms cause this to shake so that it directs the grain into the centre hole – or *eye* – of the runner stone. The contraption that causes the shoe to shake, incidentally, is called a *damsel* – apparently so called because it chatters constantly and was said to be one of the

noisiest mechanisms in the mill!

The mill stones must never touch when the top one is revolving – if they did, the friction would cause sparks, which in a building the major part of which was generally wood, was obviously hazardous. The art of milling is to get the stones as close together as possible without them touching; the further apart they are the coarser the grinding will be and the grittier the flour.

As grain is directed between the stones, the revolutions of the runner stone (the bottom, or *bed*, stone, remains stationary) begin to crush it and drive it outwards. The top surface of the runner stone and the bottom surface of the bed stone are etched with channels, which have a cutting edge and a shallower edge and fine striations, known as *stitching*. Gradually the grain is crushed and ground ever finer, during which process it gradually works its way to the edge of the stones. The stones are enclosed, usu-

Above: Early sails comprised a wooden frame over which canvas was stretched. Later sails with shutters were introduced; here you can see the mechanism used to open and close the shutters according to the wind strength.

Overleaf: The open trestle-type mill at Chillenden, Kent was one of the last mills to be built in south-east England.

usually in a wooden case, or *vat*, of some sort. Brushes round the edge sweep the floor to a chute from where it will fall into a collecting bin.

The miller tests the flour as it first falls into the bin to make sure he has the setting of his stones correct by feeling it between his finger and thumb and also by smelling it. Obviously he can feel how smooth or gritty it is easily enough; if the stones are too close together it 'burns' the flour which gives a distinctive smell.

When the stones are working, it is essential that they are kept supplied with grain. Should it run out at any times, it is possible that the sharp edges on the two stones would strike against one another, which, again, would produce sparks. The mechanism that alerts the miller to the fact that grain is getting low in the hopper is one of the most simple and ingenious of all – possibly devised by a miller having watched his mill burn down!

In the hopper is a leather strap, bolted into the hopper side at one end, with a string that leads through the hopper at the other end on to a wooden arm, pivoted at one end and with a bell attached at the

Opposite: When smock and tower mills began to be widely built, different parts of the country tended to have different styles of cap. This is a typical ogee design found on the small Ellis Mill which nestles in a residential part of the city of Lincoln.

Below: This rectangular-shaped windmill cap, constructed of wooden boards, is typical of many of the smock mills found in Kent.

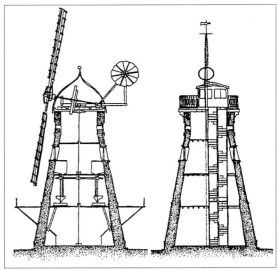

other. As long as hopper is kept supplied with grain, the leather strap is held down by its weight; as the hopper empties, the leather strap rises which releases the string, which pivots the arm – which causes the bell to ring! Providing the miller hears the bell, catastrophe can be avoided.

In its very, very simplest form that is how the windmill works to provide flour. Various other processes are, and always were, necessary. The grain, for example, generally needed to be cleaned when it arrived at the mill unless it had been previously 'threshed' to remove all the 'foreign bodies' that are present in it after harvesting. Equally when the millstones release the flour, it needs to be sifted to remove stray husks, bran and the like. Millstones had to be 'dressed' or 'redressed' quite frequently to ensure the cutting edge was kept sharp.

In the heydays of wind and water-

Top right: Diagrammatic sections through the Old Windmill in Brisbane. It was converted to a telegraph signal station in the 1860s and from 1890 to the early 1920s it was used as a Fire Brigade observation post.

mills a stone dresser was kept full employed for stones would probably need to be dressed every couple of months or so in a busy mill. Where you could possibly distinguish a miller by his dusty appearance – mills were extremely dusty places, in fact the top floor in some mills was known as the dust floor – a stone dresser was distinguishable by the little black specks on his hands. These were tiny specks of stone that gradually wore their way under his skin.

Above: An idyllic depiction of the miller at work in a long forgotten past.

Left: Sir William Cubitt, who became Lord Mayor of London, devised the patent sail.

Opposite: Shutters on a spring sail. Designed by a Scottish mill-wright at the end of the eighteenth century.

CHAPTER FOUR

WINDMILL USES

What it is that you consider to be the main work of a traditional windmill will most probably depend on where you live. In much of the western world its use is likely to be associated with the milling of flour for bread. In Holland for the first 100 years or so of the windmill's existence, this was its principal use, but in the early fifteenth century, many were

converted, and many more built, to drain the low-lying land. In Persia, where it seems windmills may have originated and in the east as they spread, their first use was to pump water for irrigation purposes. In many other places, even parts of the UK at one time, they were used to pump seawater, so that it could then be evaporated to produce salt.

Traditional windmills in USA for grinding flour were commonest along the Atlantic seaboard. Many people in the central plains, however, and also ranchers in outback Australia will primarily associate the use of wind power, and the word windmill, with the pumping of water for domestic or agricultural use. However, this is not done by the traditional grain windmill with its distinctive body and overpowering presence. Instead in mid-1800s America, there sprang up a profusion of wind-powered wheels, known as windmills and described as 'pinwheels on stilts'. They were designed to pump water from under the ground to feed the arid lands. Essentially a wheel of many

Previous pages left:
A dramatic view of a
silhouetted windmill
at sunset .

Previous pages right:
At one time these
skeleton-type wind-
mills were a common
sight in country areas
in Australia and the
USA where they were
generally used to
pump water from
the ground.

Right: An almost
painted image of
Dutch windmills sink-
ing into a misty early
evening sky.

more and much shorter blades than the sails of a traditional windmill, attached high on a tall, spindly metal structure to catch the wind, it connected to a shaft that went down into the water table. With no need to house machinery and millstones, nor little need of maintenance, the structure was minimalist and whilst it carried none of the romance of the traditional mill, it was effective, easy to produce and generally needed little maintenance.

By about 1890 there were close on 100 factories in the USA producing slight vari-

ations of design of this type of windmill, dubbed as being 'the only servant that needed no fuel, coaxing or driving'. Wealthy families bought them to provide a steady stream of running water and stockmen and homesteaders installed them to irrigate their crops and water their livestock. The spreading railway companies were the other main market, placing them along their lines to provide water to power the steam-driven locomotives.

During the centuries of domination world-wide by the traditional windmill, they were used in different places to

Above: The rusty sails of a water-pumping windmill in outback Australia.

Opposite: The distinctive five-sailed mill at Boston, Lincolnshire. Built in the early nineteenth century it is called the Maude Foster Mill and takes its name from the Maude Foster Drain which runs nearby. It is the only mill remaining of a number that used to operate in the town.

grind many substances besides flour. Cocoa, pepper, mustard, ochre – even snuff and whiting were all ground in windmills. Sugar cane growing countries used the wind-driven stones to crush the cane, while in the little squat windmills on the Greek Islands, they ground the indigenous fiva beans for local use and to sell to passing shipping.

While, it seems, that watermills were first adapted for more industrial purposes than the grinding of flour, some windmills also took over these duties. They ground bark used in tanneries for dyeing leather, or flint for making china as well as sulphur, chalk and cement clinker. Mills were adapted or designed to crush different types of seeds or nuts to produce oil.

Undoubtedly, however, one of the most monumental tasks ascribed to the traditional windmill was that of draining the low-lying land that characterised the great majority of the Netherlands. Ever fighting a losing battle against flooding in a country where much of the land lay below sea level, post mills were adapted, and then specifically built, with a scoop wheel to lift water. While this wheel had

Opposite: Built in 1814, the Union Mill at Cranbrook, Kent became so-called because it was run as a co-operative after its original owner was declared bankrupt some five years after its construction.

Below: The most famous 'windmill' in Paris, France, the Moulin Rouge is a cabaret club in the centre of the French capital, known to generations.

Above: An ochre coloured Dutch windmill melting into the countryside.

wheel would be alongside it, extending down into the water. These mills could be moved from place to place, to be employed where they were needed.

One hundred or more years later, towards the end of the sixteenth century, the huge, characteristic Dutch *polder mill* came into being. This essentially took the mechanism of a wip mill and placed it in a much larger smock mill, which often had thatched sides – thatch being a ready commodity from the reed-filled marshes. These were used now in more ambitious schemes, not merely to deal with the immediate needs of draining, but to reclaim great areas of land. Water would be lifted and put into a canal system that fed into streams, which would ultimately flow out to sea.

In draining and reclaiming land, mills would often work together, the first lifting to a certain level, where the next and then the next would take over to raise it still further. Three or four would work in close association, but along the bank of the canals there could be a long line of windmills, their sails all facing into the wind and spinning round together.

Drainage mills were also a feature of the marshy fen land of England. Although they never operated in the

to remain fixed in the water-filled basin, the mill still had to turn so that the sails faced the wind. The body was fixed on a tall wooden post and a separate drive went down to the wheel. Known as *wip mills*, a structure was built beneath the body housing the post and, very often, also the miller and his family! The scoop

numbers and scale of the Dutch mills, John Reynolds (*Windmills and Watermills, 1970*) tell us that 'fenland scenes painted in the early years of the nineteenth century shows a countryside enlivened by scores of mills'. In Norfolk, draining work was necessary to cope with land subsidence around the Broads and this was done by windmills placed at junctions of dykes and rivers.

Another common use of the windmill in Holland, and to a lesser extent in other places, was for timber – sawing. Big mills would do the work of cutting down trees, while smaller ones split timber and dealt with the lighter sawing jobs. A logical extension of this was the paper mill, again mainly found in Holland.

Coastal mills have often acted as beakers and guides to shipping, such as those in New York indicating to small craft whether it was safe to sail between there and Brooklyn. In many areas, again perhaps most notably in Holland but certainly in the UK too, the position in which the miller left the sails gave a clear message to those who knew how to read them. If a sail was left pointing straight up, it meant he expected them to be turning again soon; if both pairs were left at a 45 angle to the ground it meant that the

Above: Dumonts atmospheric turbine

mill would remain stationary for longer. The top sail stopped just before it reached the vertical and it meant that the miller was celebrating good news; stopped a bit beyond the vertical and he was in mourning.

Millers could also put their sails in a position that indicated 'lameness' – that

is the mill was not working because of some problem rather than because the miller felt like having the day off. Not only did this give a message to those who might want to use the mill, it was also hoped the millwright would 'read' it and come to repair the damage!

In the world wars of this century, the Dutch developed a warning system using their windmill, the position of the sails telling of imminent invasion. This,

of course, led to them being targets for bombs and artillery and many were demolished. In the marshy lands around the Kent coast in England, the tall windmills gave an excellent view of the surrounding countryside and many were used as lookout posts, particularly by the Home Guard. Much, much more than the process of milling flour was lost as windmills began and continued their decline.

Above: Bradwell tower mill in Milton Keynes. This was built at the beginning of the nineteenth century just after the construction of the Grand Junction Canal, now known as the Grand Union Canal, had opened up the possibility of wide trading. The mill was built with locally quarried limestone.

Opposite: A well preserved stone windmill.

WINDMILL RESTORATION

For 700 years in Europe traditional windmills reigned, turning out flour for man's most basic daily sustenance. One hundred years ago, they would still have been a common sight around the countryside; then, in less than a century, they all but disappeared, together most likely, with the true art of milling. In the UK a few

remain scattered here and there, some preserved inside and out – occasionally able to function but more frequently standing as museum pieces. A few are restored externally only, some are converted to dwellings and many more stand as little more than empty shells in various stages of disrepair and decay. Only a handful could still operate and the number that do so commercially would be counted on the fingers of two, if not one, hand.

To give an idea of how many windmills once dominated the countryside, in their heyday there were upwards of 10,000 at work in the UK. The Fens area had 2000 alone draining the land. In just one district of the Netherlands, the Zaan, more than 900 windmills were busy daily and it was estimated that there was at least one grinding mill – and possibly more – for every 2000 people throughout Holland.

It is a sad fact that probably most things begin their decline when they are actually at their peak, in terms of design and efficiency. The windmill

Above: Standing high on a hill in Washington, West Sussex, considerable changes have been made to this mill in converting it to a private home.

Previous page right: The extremely picturesque brick-built tower mill on the north Norfolk coast at Cley-next-the-Sea.

Previous page left: Forbidding on a bleak, wet day, the black smock mill at Stelling Minnis, south-east Kent is still in working order.

was no exception; with sails, mechanisms and construction all at their pinnacle, increasing industrialisation yet began to undermine its existence.

The initial signs of this came at the very end of the eighteenth century when the first flour mill in England successfully substituted steam power for wind power. Steam mills first made their appearance at the country's major ports. Here they powered rollers which ground grain brought in from overseas producing a finer, whiter flour than the hitherto commoner stoneground product of the windmill. The craving for whiter than white bread began!

Over the next century many millers installed steam and then gas powered engines in their windmills, generally as an auxiliary source of power, something that could be relied upon when the wind was at its most fickle. Still their decline through the nineteenth century was slow – wind after all has always been a free source of power, and, as such, was not so easily relinquished.

The rapid decline came at the beginning of this century; not only were alternative sources of reliable power more readily available, motor transport was also beginning to disseminate the sought-after roller-ground flour to coun-

try districts. Agricultural depression and the movement from country areas into towns spurred on the demise of windmills to the extent that it has been estimated they were falling out of use at the rate of about one a month in the UK between the two world wars. By 1945 there were virtually no working windmills in existence.

Fortunately, however, by this time in many places in the world, individuals and organisations had realised that they were losing these beautiful and now historic buildings at a fearsome rate. The Dutch, for example, have worked hard to preserve a large number of their windmills and have an association that is involved solely with windmills. In the UK, The Society for the Preservation of Ancient Buildings became involved in the preservation and restoration of windmills and watermills, and has done much to ensure their continued existence.

To some extent controversy rages over how windmills should be preserved. Many windmill enthusiasts want to see them restored faithfully to as original a state as possible, using the correct materials – the right sort of wood, correct joints between timbers and total fidelity to original construction. Frequently, however, the cost of such repair, let alone the craftsmen

Above: The famous Jack and Jill windmills on top of the Sussex Downs above Brighton. Jack – one of the few 'male' windmills – is a tower mill that became famous as the converted home of golfing correspondent, Henry Longhurst. Jill – a post mill – is the older of the two, built in the early nineteenth century close by before being moved to her present site.

to undertake it, are in short supply. Many windmills fell victim to the ravages of weather and neglect – wood that formed the main part of so many windmills rots quickly in such circumstances – before funds and enthusiasm were available for their repair.

In many places in the world windmills have been converted to houses – another form of 'preservation' that is anathema to many enthusiasts, in spite of the fact that it means a windmill that

might otherwise have been destroyed is instead saved. An example of this abhorrence led to the best of all possible results, however; on the marshy lands of eastern Kent a deserted windmill with planning permission for a house came up for sale in 1985. A local resident named Malcolm Hobbs was so appalled at the idea of the windmill being thus converted that he bought it and set about restoring it. By 1991 restoration was completed and before long it was up and running as

Above: Two spectacular windmills at Zaanse-schans, Holland.

Opposite: Trader Mill, Sibsey, Lincolnshire. This is one of the few six-sailed mills that remain in existence in England.

a commercially working mill, producing stoneground flour wholly by wind power, which sells to bakeries as well as to the public. The sight of its sails turning rhythmically in the wind is in strange juxtaposition to one of the first skeletal wind turbines that sits – now stationary – just across the marshes from it.

In terms of windmills as dwelling, however, there is, when all is said and done, really nothing new about this. Millers and their families may well have lived in the lower floors of some of the higher smock and tower mills in the UK; in Holland the accommodation was always an integral part of the huge polder mills, the sails set above the balcony or staging that marked the division between the living and working areas. With four or more floors of the mill itself and just as many for the miller and the family, it is easy to see why these buildings were such a dominating part of the landscape. In the UK there is one windmill – on the coast near Dover, in the south east – that was built in 1929 as a house and never as a working mill at all.

Amongst the most famous conversions of a windmill to a house is the one up on England's Sussex Down. Known as Jack, it has the distinction, therefore,

Left: A simple setting for a typical scene of a Dutch windmill by the side of a waterway.

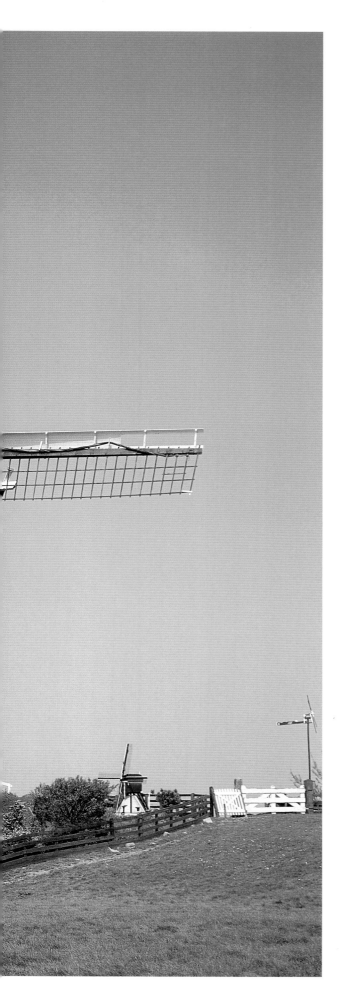

of being one of the few male windmills. It is a black tower mill that stands next door to an older post mill, appropriately called Jill, and was apparently built in the late 1860s to replace a post mill that had previously stood there. It became famous as the house of Henry Longhurst, of golfing reknown.

By and large it is mainly tower mills that have sufficient space to turn them into houses although a few smock mills have been converted. One of the major problems with six to eight-sided smock mills is that rain can be extremely persistent in finding its way through the joints and crevices. In all windmills it is also likely to run down the sails and through the centre of the windshaft. Many tower mills were built with windows set directly above one another, itself an inherent construction weakness which caused the towers to cave in as a result.

Doubtless the controversy of whether a windmill should be converted or not is one that will continue to rage. Done sensitively, however, it does seem a way of preserving at least some of these historic buildings, of preventing them otherwise disappearing for ever.

Left: A beautiful Dutch windmill framed against a summer sky.

CHAPTER SIX

WINDMILLS TOMORROW

Not much more than a century ago, nearly every industrial process in existence ran on wind power. In his book *Technological Self-Sufficiency* (1976), Robin Clarke says, "Wind and water power catered for all men's energy needs for about 99.99 per cent of human history" and goes on to prophesy that "wind power will certainly be back with us in a big way by the next century".

Wind power has never entirely been abandoned. While the great, traditional windmills fell out of use in many areas, ousted by steam, gas and finally electricity, they remained in use in their more skeletal form in many outback areas of USA and Australia and across much of the less developed world to pump water. This could be stored in tanks for later use, so the fact that the windmills worked only when the wind was blowing mattered less than in the grinding mills. In addition, particular throughout the USA, these windmills were also used to generate electricity. Then in the 1930s the building of more central generating plants took electricity way into the rural areas and the use even of these windmills began to decline.

Still there was an interest in harnessing the wind and using it as a source of energy. Experiments were undertaken with wind 'mills' or machines of all sorts, many of which could be homemade and were used to generate electricity on a domestic scale. One of the commonest of these

was the Savonius rotor – invented in 1922 by a Finnish engineer, SJ Savonius. It consisted of semi-circular blades, welded together to make an S-shape and in its simplest form, it could be made by cutting an oil drum in half vertically and welding the two halves together in this configuration. Another with a more industrial application was the Darrieus turbine, patented by a French engineer, G Darrieus – its two or three thin metal blades bowed out in the middle and were joined at the top and bottom to a shaft so that the whole thing resembled a giant egg beater.

For long the biggest wind machine known to man was one built on a mountain in Vermont, USA. It comprised two blades, weighing eight tons, with a blade width of 4.8 metres (16ft) at their widest and stretching 53 metres (175ft) from tip to tip. It was able to pump sufficient electricity into the local grid to power a community of about 200 homes, until coming to an untimely end when one of the blades tore loose.

At this time fuel was cheap and nuclear energy was beginning to be used. Amidst this 'Brave New World' atmosphere, general experimentation on wind machines slowed for a couple of decades. Then came the 1970s with its oil short-

ages – a major source of fuel with any number of applications. People woke up again to the fact that using the wind to generate electricity – ironically one of the powers that had ultimately helped in the demise of the windmill – was to use a free commodity that did not threaten the earth's dwindling resources or bring with it any harmful effects. One source has estimated that if we could use 0.5 per cent of the wind flowing round our planet, we would generate more energy than the whole of the human race currently uses.

Experiments moved on to the modern wind turbine – essentially the 'windmills' of the second half of the twentieth century. These tend to have from one to four metal blades, each one twisted like an aeroplane propeller, which they somewhat resemble. The one that is probably most widely used was the three-bladed type, known as Jacobs three-bladed windmill after its inventor Marcellus Jacobs.

Although there are numbers of examples of individual wind turbines or small clusters grouped together providing electricity for individual homes or a modest community, there are growing numbers of instances of the turbines being installed in profusion in what have become to be known as 'wind farms'.

These supply electricity direct to the national grid. The first of these to be built in the UK was Delabole wind farm, near Tintagel, Cornwall, where the annual production of electricity is equivalent to the energy needs for 3000 households. Since its construction in 1991, Cumbria, Norfolk, Yorkshire, Northumberland, Lancashire, Tyne and Wear, Gloucestershire, Wales and parts of Ireland have all 'sprouted' wind farms. The largest currently in the UK is the Llandinam wind farm in mid-Wales, which has more than 100 x 300kW wind turbines and has a production that almost doubles any other.

Wind farms have undoubtedly gained more and more ground since their inception around the beginning of the 1990s, in spite of frequent opposition from local communities who consider them both an eyesore and unacceptably noisy. Huge farms have been installed in the USA notably in Palm Springs, California, where, beginning in 1994, the installation has since been undertaken in stages. Denmark is one of the countries in the forefront of this development and was the first to pioneer wind farms off-shore, beginning with the Vindeby wind farm in the Baltic Sea off the southern part of the country. Offshore wind farms are much costlier to construct, but their energy production is also higher. Many people consider them to be the way ahead in countries where a high population density makes it correspondingly difficult to find land sites.

It is undoubtedly the feeling of many that wind power must once again be exploited on a large scale as we move towards the 21st century. Whilst modern wind turbines have not the aesthetic beauty of the great traditional windmills of the past, they undoubtedly owe a debt to them Take heed of this quote from the *New York Times* of February 1971 by a former Secretary of State, "Windmills are much, much more than relics. They are symbols of sanity for a world that is increasingly hooked on machines with an inordinate hunger for fuel and a prodigious capacity to pollute. The issue is nobler than survival; it is whether we can equip ourselves to live truly decent lives. If we are to meet this challenge our inventors and technicians will have to pay homage to windmills; they will have to build machines that use and not abuse the unearned gifts of nature."

It is a fitting tribute to the windmills of our past.

INDEX